Strange Tales of North-East Scotland

LOCHNAGAR.

Introduction

What is the grim truth about witchcraft in Old Aberdeen? Where did a castle laird rise from the grave? Why was hot molten gold poured down a tradesman's throat? How did Satanic rituals in Nairn district lead to death? What happened when a phantom appeared in an Aberdeen house after a servant hanged herself? Why did a well of 'miracle water' get Elgin folk into trouble?

These are just some of the many questions answered in the collection of fascinating legends, stories and reports which make up "Strange Tales of North-East Scotland."

You can also find out about:- The 'Braemar Sacrifice' which forced a young lad to shoot an arrow at his mother; the Nairn ghost with no hands; the spine-chilling events which followed the appearance of a child corpse in an Aberdeen hotel; the 27 people who were burned alive as an act of revenge; the murdered girl who literally terrified her killer to death; Braemar's family of ghosts; the guilty secrets of Banffshire's Green Lady; the miracle which played a key role in bringing Christianity to Deeside; the castle of headless ghosts; the two men who had to face a murder trial after statements from a phantom; an Aberdeenshire family's death curse; the water-kelpie who drowned folk in the River Spey; the helpful spirit of the Dee; and so on.

The engravings of local scenes in days gone by were first published in "Scottish Pictures" (1866) by Samuel G. Green.

Illustrations by John Mackay.

FRONT COVER: Banffshire's Green Lady.
BACK COVER: Cawdor Castle, Nairn.
DRAWING: The Nairn Confessions.

First published 1978. Reprinted 1979, 1980, 1982, 1984, 1987, 1988, 1990.
ISBN No. 0946264 66 X

Dead man's gold

Dead Man's Gold

A fourteenth century blacksmith called Osbarn was one of the North-East's most evil sons. His treachery and lust for money led to an entire garrison of his countrymen being butchered by the English in September, 1306.

Osbarn was a blacksmith serving the little community of Greenstyle, nestling on the southern slopes of Ben Newe, and the mighty castle of Kildrummy. Business was excellent and he made handsome profits attending to the military horses and other needs at the castle.

But Osbarn, a greedy selfish character who didn't have a friend in the world, was always trying to make more and more money. He wanted to be one of the richest men in the kingdom and was determined that nothing and no one would stop him reaching his goal.

In the summer of 1306 certain events occurred which were to drastically affect his life and those of many others. King Robert the Bruce had been defeated at Methven near Perth. He managed to flee and make for Aberdeen. There Robert was met by the Queen, daughter Marjorie and brother Nigel. Other Scots swelled the numbers of the Royal party but it was forced to move west because of the continuing advance of the English.

As the days passed Robert came to the conclusion that the struggle was going to be very bitter and tough so he sent the ladies to Kildrummy Castle for safety under the escort of Nigel and the Earl of Atholl. However bad news awaited the party there when it was learned that Edward of Carnarvon, son of the infamous Edward I of England, was heading north. The Queen and her ladies fled to the sanctuary of St. Duthac's Chapel at Tain. Nigel Bruce stayed behind to lead the defence against the enemy.

Plans were made to deal with the attack and Osbarn was kept busy checking all the ironwork of the castle. Any weak points in this area would give the English an obvious advantage.

On August 1 Edward set up camp at Kildrummy. Then the campaign to storm it began. Attack followed attack but the brave Scots stood firm. The days turned into weeks and still the English couldn't make any headway.

All this time our greedy blacksmith was busy planning and plotting. If the English won the garrison would surely be put to the sword and that would be the end of his business. If they lost things would revert to the status quo and he would be no better off. So, in an attempt to drastically alter the situation, Osbarn sneaked out of the castle late one night and headed for the English camp. He explained his business to a soldier and was taken to meet the Prince. The English then devised a plan on how to seize Kildrummy with his assistance. But the smith was a bit put out when it emerged that part of the scheme would involve him setting it on fire. He hadn't planned on having to do anything which might be so risky. Osbarn demanded a suitable reward and let out a howl of delight when Edward told him: "You will have as much gold as you can carry." All he had to do was return to the castle and await the signal to start the fire.

This came a few days later and Osbarn threw a piece of red hot metal on to the thatched roof of the great hall which was situated near to his forge. The flames spread very quickly and the garrison was thrown into a state of total confusion. The brave Scots, once they had recovered from the initial shock, managed to seal up the openings caused by the fire. Unfortunately their food and ammunition had been destroyed in the blaze. So tragically it was hunger and not the English which forced them to surrender in early September.

Nigel Bruce was hanged at Berwick and the rest of the garrison were all butchered. Proud as a peacock Osbarn went to claim his reward. But a big shock was in store. The English tied him up, forced open his mouth and poured molten gold down his throat. They had kept their word. The greedy smith got as much gold as he could carry...

Blown-up?

In the fifteenth century did the people of Braemar turn cannons on Kindrochit Castle in the village, blasting it and all the occupants inside to pieces? According to tradition locals had become terrified after hearing about the outbreak of a deadly plague within the castle walls.

They were determined that it would not spread. Barricades were put up to trap the garrison inside and cannons were brought over from Atholl to blow Kindrochit and the killer disease sky-high. In later years there were stories of ghosts sitting around a huge table in the vaults.

All around were skulls and mountains of treasure. Such a scene was vividly described by a Hanoverian soldier who had been lowered down there in 1746 to try and find treasure. He was absolutely petrified and vowed never to go near the place again.

At least that's the story. All we can really be certain of is that in 1400 Kindrochit was a place of great hustle and bustle and full of life. Just 100 years later it was completely abandoned and in decay.

Earlier this century serious excavation work was carried out and after a great deal of hard toil the walls of the main part of the old castle were uncovered. Amongst the many finds was the famous silver gilt Kindrochit brooch.

BALMORAL FROM THE MEADOWS.

The Braemar sac

The Braemar Sacrifice

Hundreds of years ago in Braemar, the Castle of Kindrochit was a popular residence for Scottish Kings who came to the North on hunting expeditions. Constables who governed it had considerable feudal powers over the local population and the incumbent of the post during Malcolm Canmore's time chose to exercise his authority in a somewhat peculiar fashion. Families were ordered to provide him with a live cow on a rota basis which he used to feed a wild boar.

The beast, kept as the castle 'pet', was called Tad-Losgann and was a great source of amusement to Malcolm during his frequent visits...particularly as it had always grown quite considerably!

Farmers in the area, who at the best of times had a terrible struggle to make ends meet, bitterly resented this plunder of their stock but were powerless to act. Then one day something happened which so to speak was the straw to break the camel's back. Sandy McLeod, a lad of some 15 summers and much respected bowman throughout the district, was very angry when the Constable chose his widowed mother's cow to feed Tad-Losgann. In hard financial terms it represented more than two years solid work and she was heartbroken by the decision. Neighbours could only offer sympathy but Sandy decided on a positive course of action. He would kill the beast!

Later that night and outwith his mother's knowledge he made a set of special arrows. After dawn part one of his plan was implemented when the first arrow was used to shoot a large capercailzie. This was to be the bait which would draw Tad-Losgann from his den.

Sandy hid the capercailzie near his home until nightfall. Then after darkness he set out. The young archer skilfully avoided being seen by the castle guard and once within shooting distance of the den he hurled his carcase towards the boar. Hours seemed to pass and nothing happened. Then Tad-Losgann appeared and followed the scent. Within a few seconds Sandy had the perfect shot and without hesitating he fired. The arrow went straight through the beast's heart. Death was instant. Sandy managed to get back to his mother's cottage in Glen Slugan without being spotted. Once inside he collapsed into a deep sleep totally exhausted.

Next morning the news spread like wildfire and local folk, delighted at the end of the cow sacrifices, hailed the mystery killer as a hero. The Constable was, of course, not amused. He ordered a search of every home in the district. The arrow taken from Tad-Losgann's heart was matched up with arrows found in the McLeod cottage. Sandy was taken prisoner and confessed to the 'crime'. He was sentenced to die on the gallows on Creag Choinnich the following morning.

Coincidentally the king was due to arrive for a visit at around the same time. The Widow McLeod was heartbroken and blamed herself for all that had happened. She decided that a reprieve from the king was their only hope and set out to meet the Royal party. Malcolm, when he heard what the widow had to say, promised to make enquiries on his arrival at Kindrochit. After hearing the facts he decided that Sandy should have a chance of life. His mother was to be put on a rocky ledge across from the castle with a peat balanced on her head. If he could pierce it from the castle drawbridge freedom would be the prize. The lad was trembling with fear but knew this was his only hope.

The Widow McLeod smiled at her son and gave him as much encouragement as she could. Sandy took aim...fired...and knocked the peat off her head. The watching crowd gave squeals of delight and King Malcolm congratulated the lad on a "splendid" shot. He also promised Sandy a place in the Royal Archers when a man. But this was not to be for young McLeod never fired another arrow in the rest of his long lifetime.

THE "CAULDRON;" BULLERS OF BUCHAN.

A Slave's Curse

When Andrew Lammie and Agnes Smith met it was love at first sight. Sadly however for them a happy marriage and children were not to be. For Agnes was the daughter of a very wealthy and proud local miller who wanted her to wed someone rich and influential. Andrew was as poor as a church mouse and his job of trumpeter at Fyvie Castle, Aberdeenshire, in the eighteenth century, didn't offer any prospect of sudden prosperity.

The miller banned the young couple's courtship but they continued to meet in secret. All was well until the jealous laird of Fyvie stepped in. He too had fallen for the miller's daughter but she'd spurned his advances. This was more than the laird could take and he decided to hit back after hearing about the meetings by having Andrew transported to the West Indies as a slave!

The young trumpeter lived and worked there in wretched conditions but after a few years he managed to escape and made his way back to Scotland. Never a day had passed without the love of his life being in his thoughts.

Sadly, however, she was not there when he came home. Agnes had died of a broken heart during his absence. The strain of getting back coupled with the long hours of toil as a slave had taken their toll on Andrew. Once strong and firm he was now weak and the tragic news drained from him the will to live.

A short time later he died and on his deathbed cursed the Laird of Fyvie, swearing that a trumpet would sound every time a laird was about to die. The story goes that the haunting of Fyvie began a short time later and for many years afterwards the death of a laird was preceded by a trumpet blast in the stillness of the night.

Another ghost which has been linked with Fyvie in the past is that of a Green Lady but her origins were a mystery.

This fourteenth century castle has an interesting story to tell about the famous Scots wizard Thomas the Rhymer. He cursed all future owners after being refused a night's shelter there by declaring that the place would never descend in direct line for more than two generations.

The man who whipped up the wizard's anger was Sir Henry Preston of Craigmillar, the then owner, and a noted participant in the battle of Otterburn (1388). He was upset on the day of the Rhymer's visit over demolition work which had gone wrong and snapped that no room was available when the request was made for accommodation. As it happened a small crowd, familiar with the great reputation which Thomas had in matters magic, had gathered outside the castle to see him. Now they were given first hand experience of him working a curse!

The black colonel

The sky turned black and the clear sunny day gave way to a terrible thunderstorm. The wind howled around the castle and everyone watching got a real soaking. Yet the spot where Thomas stood remained bone dry and there wasn't a speck of rain on him.

From what is known of owners in the few centuries that followed it would seem that his curse operated effectively.

He rose from the Grave

John Farquharson, one of the seventeenth century chiefs of Inverey Castle, was known as "The Black Colonel" because he was a tall dark man and a fearless fighter.

One of the proudest moments of his life came with the Battle of Killiecrankie when he raised a small army to fight alongside Viscount Dundee. Many of his men died but the Black Colonel managed to escape and flee back to Inverey with the Redcoats in hot pursuit. He cleverly sidetracked up Glen Ey and took shelter in a cottage while the enemy tried to storm the castle. Eventually they got inside and were furious to learn that Farquharson had evaded them. As a 'punishment' the building was set on fire and the chief's retainers were all butchered.

The Black Colonel however had the last word. Before going into battle he had filled a room with gunpowder and as the fire spread there was a mighty explosion which blew many of the Redcoats to pieces. Later after gathering more men the Black Colonel took the remainder of the enemy on in a skirmish at Braemar. He won and they were driven from the district.

But Farquharson was not content with simply being a controversial and colourful figure in life. Even after death he still made his presence felt.

The story goes that the Colonel's final wish was to be buried in the family graveyard at Inverey. Well-meaning folk however decided that he should go to his last resting place with chieftain's honours at Castleton of Braemar.

This was done but the day after the funeral puzzled passers-by found the coffin lying beside the grave which only hours earlier had been filled in. Three times the coffin was buried. And three times it mysteriously rose. His followers decided to take it to Inverey. The road was blocked because of a landslide so a raft was made to float it down the Dee. He was laid to rest in the family graveyard and there was never again any trouble from the Black Colonel.

Water of Miracles

A Celtic missionary called St. Monire played a key role in bringing the message of Christianity to Deeside. But he nearly died after being viciously beaten up by the simple natives who lived in the hamlet of Auchendryne where he had gone to spread the word of God. They had been told by their pagan priest that St. Monire was an evil spirit who could cause great trouble if allowed to stay. This terrified the locals who attacked the missionary with sticks and stones.

Saddened and badly bruised St. Monire fled for his life. He travelled along the banks of the Dee and by nightfall had reached Inverey. Unfortunately word from the pagan priest got there before he did with the result that his requests for a little food and shelter against the bitterly cold night were refused.

The missionary was an elderly man who had been advised by friends not to make the hazardous journey into the wilds of Aberdeenshire and now he was beginning to think that they were probably right. St. Monire decided to press on but on the slopes of Càrn Na' Moine collapsed from sheer exhaustion. Death seemed inevitable and the next morning he could hardly move at all.

The pagan priest, who was hiding near by, watched cheerfully as the dying Christian groaned in agony. Then a miracle happened. A stream of sparkling clear water began flowing out of the rocky hillside. St. Monire crawled towards it and began drinking. With each mouthful he grew stronger and stronger. A few minutes later St. Monire was as fit as a fiddle!

The pagan priest then appeared and declared: "That stream will be cursed as it has fed the thirst of an evil spirit!" He called on the Pagan Gods to dry it up and threw mud on to the source to stop it flowing. The stream vanished.

St. Monire calmly replied that it had been blessed in the name of the Virgin Mary, said a short prayer and the water began bubbling forth again. The priest was astonished and begged forgiveness. St. Monire had won his first convert. For centuries afterwards folk who were sick and ill came from all over to partake of the water and many cures were claimed because of its magical properties.

After turning Auchendryne into a Christian community St. Monire moved on to Crathie where he built a church. Following his death in 824 an annual fair was started in his honour and held on December 18 each year. St. Monire also worked among the people of Balvenie in Banffshire where a church was built.

ater of miracles

A child corpse

A Child Corpse

In the early 1900s a baffling ghost story unfolded in an elegant hotel situated near Aberdeen's St. Swithin's Street. One of the rooms was occupied by a tourist who was dying slowly and painfully from what a doctor described as "a very loathsome Oriental disease fortunately rare in this country." All the hotel staff knew about her was that she had at one time been an actress and had arrived at the hotel while suffering the first effects of the illness. She registered under the name "Miss Vining."

A certain Nurse MacKenzie was called in to look after Miss Vining's needs. The hotel itself had been recently modernised and the new decor impressed the nurse. But when she entered Miss Vining's room there seemed to be a dramatic change in the atmosphere. Nurse MacKenzie suddenly felt very depressed and downhearted yet there was nothing concrete to account for her feelings. The same thing happened when she went on duty at 8 p.m. the following evening. It was a wild and stormy night outside and Nurse MacKenzie decided to pass the time by reading. Two hours later she looked up from her book and was surprised to see a small girl sitting on the chair beside Miss Vining's bed. Assuming that the child had slipped in unnoticed the nurse was about to ask her to leave when the child raised a hand. This seemed to cast a spell over our Florence Nightingale who now takes up the story....

"She motions me back. I obey because I cannot help myself. Her action is accompanied by an unpleasantly peculiar expression that holds me spellbound....

"Her face turns towards Miss Vining, but she wears a very wide-brimmed hat and I can see nothing of her features. I gather she is both beautiful and aristocratic. Something in her serpent-like ease suggests the East...."

Meantime Miss Vining was rolling about the bed going through terrible physical and mental torture. Her temperature had shot up to an alarming 104. Then the child suddenly vanished.

On the third night Nurse MacKenzie was given strict instructions not to allow any visitors so she locked the door behind her and settled down by the fire. Aberdeen was again bitterly cold and the streets outside were covered in snow. The nurse was glad to be indoors and feeling snug and warm she began to doze off. But sobbing from the bed jolted her awake. The child was there again and held up her hand towards Nurse MacKenzie who collapsed "spellbound and paralysed" as her patient moaned in terror. When the child walked towards the window a few minutes later the spell appeared to be broken. The nurse now demanded to know who she was. There was no reply and Nurse MacKenzie snatched the wide-brimmed hat from her head.

But it just vanished into thin air. Then the nurse found herself staring into the face of a Hindu child whose throat had been cut.

Nurse MacKenzie fainted from shock. When she came round the child had gone and Miss Vining was dead.

Later the nurse looked through her patient's possessions in the hope of finding some information which might lead her to relatives who would need to be informed of the death. She was intrigued to come across a large envelope marked "Quetta". Inside was a picture of a Hindu child and Miss MacKenzie recognised the dress immediately. It was the one worn by her phantom visitor! On the back of it were the words: "Natalie, may God forgive us both."

Advertisements were placed in newspapers seeking further information but there was no response.

The Hindu child was happy with her revenge, it would seem, because no child ghosts were ever seen in the hotel after Miss Vining's death. But there were reports of a woman ghost in the building.

Charming the Rain

Throughout the North-East various ceremonies were observed to try and influence the weather by making it either rain or shine. A typical example of this from Banffshire was recorded by James Mackinlay in "Folklore of Scottish Lochs and Springs" published in 1893.

It states: "At Botriphnie, in Banffshire, six miles from Keith, the wooden image of St. Fumac used to be solemnly washed in his well on the third of May. We may conclude that the ceremony was intended as a rain-charm. It must have been successful, on at least one occasion, for the River Isla became flooded through the abundance of rain. Indeed, the flooding was so great that the saint's image was swept away by the rushing water. The image was finally stranded at Banff, where it was burned as a relic of superstition by order of the parish minister about the beginning of the present century."

The Angry Spirit

Two men had to stand trial after allegations of murder were made against them by A GHOST! They were accused of murdering an English sergeant by the name of Arthur Davies. The spirit of Davies, who had vanished while on a solo hunting trip appeared almost a year later before shepherd Alexander MacPherson. In a dramatic statement he pleaded for a decent burial and after giving the location of his remains, named his killers as Duncan Clark and Alexander Bain MacDonald.

They were both known to be Jacobite sympathisers and as such had an obvious motive. For Davies was a sergeant in the English Army and with a team of men had been sent to Aberdeen after the fiasco of the Second Jacobite Rebellion to ensure that the local Scots were kept well and truly in their place. This was done through a number of measures such as the banning of the kilt and other forms of tartan dress.

A few hours before being killed Davies, while on patrol in the Braemar district caught John Gowar of Glenchunie wearing a tartan coat. The sergeant gave Gowar a severe rocketing. It was to be his last reprimand. That same day murder struck and Davies, who always dressed well and carried plenty of money, was robbed of every penny and other items of value which were on his person.

But in death he was determined to get justice and returned to Braemar where he appeared before MacPherson. MacPherson wasn't helpful, so the sergeant then appeared before an Isobel MacHardy, who was the wife of the shepherd's employer. That started things moving. There was a proper funeral, then Clark and MacDonald were arrested. However, at their trial in Edinburgh (1754), the evidence against them, although strong, was not enough to warrant a conviction. The case ended with both men being acquitted.

Ghost of the cliffs

Ghost of the Cliffs!

Wealthy heiress Isobel Fraser was heartbroken when her father banned all contact with the man she loved. It was yet another example of the bullying which made life unpleasant for all who lived and worked some centuries ago at Wine Tower—a solid building of several storeys overlooking the North Sea near Fraserburgh. As far as the laird, Sir Alexander Fraser, was concerned he was right about everything and anyone who opposed him on a point just had to be wrong.

Isobel found life lonely and miserable until a stranger called John Crawford knocked on the door one evening. Outside a snowstorm was in full blast and the visitor explained to the doorman that he had been en route to visit relatives when his horse went lame.

Isobel's father was away on business for a few days and she gave instructions to servants that Mr Crawford was to be given food and shelter. Later they met for a chat and Isobel was surprised to find herself face to face with a handsome young man of around her own age. They got on very well and talked long into the night. This was just the first of many meetings and their friendship grew into love. But all dates had to be conducted in secret because Sir Alexander disapproved of the young man.

One day, however, he received information about a rendezvous and locked Isobel in her room. His men were then sent off to arrest John who was put in chains in a cave below the tower.

That night the sea was very stormy and water which swept into the bleak 'dungeon' drowned the prisoner. Next morning, unaware of the tragedy, Sir Alexander, took Isobel down to the cave. He wanted to teach them both a lesson by showing who was boss. Inside they found the cold and lifeless body.

It would be an understatement to describe the scene which followed as an angry one. Isobel accused her father of many things, including murder. She then went up to the top of the tower and jumped off...drowning in the sea below. Sir Alexander never recovered from the double tragedy which his actions had produced and became a virtual recluse for the rest of his life.

The story has one final twist. It is said that these events are not unconnected with the appearance, from time to time, of a phantom who roams the clifftops stopping every so often to listen to the sounds of the birds and of the sea....

Ghosts with no hands or hea[ds]

No Hands or Heads

The ruined Rait Castle near Nairn is believed by some to be haunted by the ghost of a girl who has no hands and wears a blood-stained dress. She is a daughter of the Cummings family who were the owners at one time.

A bright, intelligent girl she was very much in love with a member of the Mackintosh family. Unfortunately they were despised by her father who had hatched a plot to lure his enemies to a banquet and once inside Rait murdered them all. The plan came unstuck and the girl was accused of tipping off her lover.

As a punishment for this alleged 'betrayal' the chief of the Cummings family cut off both his daughter's hands. The poor girl was at her wits end and the sheer horror of what had happened drove her to suicide.

Down through the centuries there have been occasional glimpses of her troubled spirit moving amongst the ruins.

Ghosts with no heads have been reported at Dunphail Castle, south of Forres. One of them is the spirit of an Alastair Cummings, who along with several companions, managed to escape from the fortress while it was being besieged by the Earl of Moray.

Later they succeeded in getting supplies of meal into the castle to feed the starving clansmen within. Sadly, the daring heroes were captured and beheaded. Their heads were thrown over the castle wall by Moray's men who cried: "Here's beef for your bannocks!"

Years later during excavation of a nearby mound, five headless skeletons were found.

During 1571 Corgarff Castle, some 15 miles north-west of Ballater, was the scene of mass murder. While her husband was away, the mistress, Margaret Forbes, plus 26 relatives and servants were burned to death in a retaliatory raid by the Gordons.

Not surprisingly the 16th century tower house, converted into a garrison post and enclosed within a star-shaped wall in 1748, was said to be a haunted place after that.

James VI regarde
a great pleasure t
attend trials...

The Aberdeen Witches

The persecution of witches was carried out with appalling ferocity during two and a half centuries of Scottish history. Thousands of people were tortured, then burned, between 1479 and 1722.

Barbaric methods were used to obtain confessions from suspects. Branding with hot irons, pressing of thumbs and legs in vices, and forcing victims to wear iron boots which were alternately heated and cooled, were among the least of the harrowing ordeals inflicted by well meaning but dreadfully misguided churchmen.

Innocent folk could be strangled and burned solely on the word of an enemy. Even a king like James VI regarded it a great pleasure to attend trials.

Aberdeen suffered an attack of "witch fever" in the late 1590s. The year 1594 saw several women being sent to their deaths at the stake. In 1596-97, no fewer than 24 women and two men died as a result of executions or tortures. These unfortunate people had been held prisoners in the kirk. Two women died before being brought to trial. Cause: Starvation and continual prodding with sharp stakes.

Locals were pleased. An entry in the Council Register of September 21, 1597, states: "The quhilk day, the prowest, baillies and counsell, considering that William Dun, dean of gild, has deligentlie and cairfillie dischargit him of hes office of deanrie of gild, and hes painfullie travellit(laboured) theirin to the advancing of the commoun gude, and besyddes this, hes extraordinarlie takin panis on the birning of the gryt number of witches brint this yeir, and in the four pirrattis, and bigging of the port on the brig of Dee, reparing of the Greyfreris kirk and stepill thairof, and thairby hes ben abstractit fra hes tred of merchandice continewallie...theirfoir in recompence of hes extraordinarie panis and in satisfactioun theirof (not to induce any preparative to deanes of gild to crave a recompance heirefter) but to incurage utheris to travell als diligentlie in the discharge of their office, grantit and assignit to him the soume of fourtie-seven pundis thrie s. four d. awand be him of the rest of his compt. of the unlawis (fines) of the persons convict for slaying of blakfische (kelts) and dischargit him theirof be thir presentis for ever."

Charges brought against witches in old Aberdeen were wide-ranging. They included dancing with the devil round the market cross, using supernatural powers to make husbands unfaithful to their wives, and developing a potion which rendered other victims impotent.

Janet Wishart, an elderly soul who died in the flames, was accused of casting spells on an Alexander Thomson and an Andrew Webster. Both men had complained of suffering from severe fits of shivering followed by fits of sweating. Webster eventually died from the effects. Besides this the indictment against Wishart made reference to numerous other unspecified deaths as well as acts of witchcraft which included using burning coals to raise storms and of creating monster cats to frighten chosen victims.

A woman named Isobel Crocker was burned along with Wishart. Old records detail the costs of execution:-

Item:
For 20 loads of peat to burn them	40 shillings.
For a boll (six bushels) of coal	24 shillings.
For 4 tar barrels	26 shillings 8 pence.
For fir and iron barrels	16 shillings 8 pence.
For a stake and dressing of it	16 shillings.
For four fathoms of tows(hangman's rope)	4 shillings
For carrying the peat, coals and barrels to the hill	8 shillings 4 pence.
To one justice for their execution	13 shillings 4 pence.

There is one final irony to the burnings. Because of the high costs of arranging such executions—around £350 in today's terms—many of the victims had to pay towards the costs.

Back from the Dead

A voice came back from the dead, helped cure a young man of a terminal disease, and made a well near Cromarty famous as a watering-hole where the sick could go and be cured. The well became known as Fiddler's Well after William Fiddler made a miraculous recovery from consumption. He and a friend had been seized by the condition at the same time. The second young man died soon afterwards and William, who by now was wasted away to a shadow, needed every ounce of strength he could muster to attend the funeral.

That night he had great difficulty in getting to sleep. The loss of his best pal and the pain within his own body combined to make rest very difficult. It was only after many hours of tossing and turning that he eventually fell into a deep sleep. The peace was broken by a dream in which his departed companion asked William to go to a spot on the outskirts of the town. William arose from his bed, still sleeping, and walked there. At the appointed rendezvous he sat down and a few minutes later a bee started buzzing around his head. The buzzing seemed to take on the voice of his dead companion and it was saying: "Dig, Willie, and drink! Dig, Willie, and drink!"

William obeyed the command and no sooner had he torn the first sod than a spring of clear water gushed from the hollow. Next day he returned to the spot—this time wide awake—and drank from the spring. It restored him to full health.

Hugh Miller in "Scenes and Legends of the North of Scotland", a most fascinating old book, says: "Its virtues are still celebrated, for though the water be only simple water it must be drank in the morning, and as it gushes from the bank; and, with pure air, exercise and early rising for its auxiliaries it continues to work cures."

The Faeries' Cradle

Our forefathers believed that the fairies took great delight in stealing newly born infants from the cradle and leaving mischievous changelings in their place. All sorts of customs and rites were adopted to try and stop this happening.

But even if the wee folk managed to beat such measures and take the child, distraught parents could always find hope at St. Bennet's Spring near Cromarty. For by passing the changeling through a trough of water there the imposter immediately vanished and their snatched child would be restored to them. The trough, known as "Fairies' Cradle" had a sudden end in 1745 when the parish minister and two elders broke it to pieces so that "it might no longer serve the purposes of superstition."

KING'S COLLEGE, ABERDEEN.

Magic Wells

In times past almost every parish in the North-East had a well which was said to possess remarkable qualities for healing this or that ailment. Our forefathers firmly believed in the reputations which had built up around certain waters and in search of a cure they ran the risk of heavy fines and humiliating public rebukes from the churches.

Christian teachers frowned upon the faith which folk placed in wells and kirk sessions, anxious to stamp out the primitive beliefs, imposed stiff penalties on those who were caught ignoring their instructions not to visit wells for the purposes of healing.

However they could not stop the steady procession of sick men and women or relatives who made pilgrimages to places like the chapel well of St. Mary's in the old parish of Dundurcus on Speyside. Its water had been famed from time immemorial as a great health giver and for 200 years after the Reformation the weak came, from Buchan in the east to the Hebrides in the west, to quench their thirsts.

Elgin parish records of the late sixteenth and much of the seventeenth centuries contain details of steps taken to deal with offenders. One man lost his job as a church official and others were fined for visiting St. Mary's. Still more pilgrims had to go through the mental agony of a verbal roasting in front of the congregation.

St. Fittack's Well, near the old church of St. Fittack's at the Bay of Nigg, south of Aberdeen, was a favourite with folk who wanted to improve their overall health by drinking the cool water. From the Reformation onwards the church tried to put an end to the visits and the kirk session of the burgh made it an offence to go to St. Fittack's "in ane superstitious manner". The town council gave their backing on May 16, 1616. A maximum £2 fine would be imposed on all heads of families, wives or children found guilty of breaking the ban. For servants the maximum penalty would be £1 payable by employers who in law were responsible for them.

Some of the cures claimed by particular wells were interesting. Whooping cough vanished instantly after a visit to a fountain near the burn of Oxhill in Rathven while the Fuaran Fiountag at Strathspey cured toothache. Skin diseases or sores were helped at Fergan's Well, Kirkmichael, Banffshire. The best times for visiting most wells were reckoned to be the first Sundays of November, February, May and August.

The Nairn confes

The Nairn Confessions

The confessions of witch Isobel Gowdie and her companions caused a sensation in the Nairn district. They named many prominent local people of the day as participants in coven rituals which had sex orgies as one of their main features.

Isobel lived in the village of Auldearn and said that she had been baptised into the black art by the Devil himself at a ceremony in the parish church. Along with her coven leader John Young she admitted casting spells over farmers' fields so that their sect would get the benefits of the crops whilst growers got nothing.

Under cross-examination by officials she explained why those women who indulged in supernatural practises were not missed by husbands when they went out in the middle of the night to attend coven meetings. The witches simply placed a broom or stool in the bed, whispered a short spell and the object took on their appearance. To reach the rendezvous point they put a straw between their feet, recited a short rhyme and flew off.

Isobel confessed to being involved in an attempt to murder the parish minister, Mr Harry Forbes, whilst he was ill. The flesh, entrails and gall of a toad, a hare's liver, grains of barley, nail parings, and bits of his clothing were all steeped in water and put in a bag. While this was being done the Devil stood chanting: "He is lying in his bed and he is sick and sore. Let him lie in that bed two months and days three more. He shall lie in his bed, he shall be sick and sore, He shall lie in his bed two months and days three more." The coven members also joined in the chant whilst on their knees and as they spoke they raised their hands towards the Devil. Bessie Hay, one of the witches, was sent into the minister's room with the bag. But good Christian folk were there visiting Mr Forbes so the spell was effectively broken.

Other admissions which were made in the year 1662 included attempts to harm the children of a local landowner, the Laird of Parks, with images. No conclusive record exists to prove whether Isobel met the usual witch death of burning at the stake but judging by her claims, whether true or imaginary, she certainly made every effort to achieve just that!

Lady Agnes snatched it from his hand

Revenge of a Poisoned Girl

An intriguing story lies behind the reported sighting once a year of a female phantom who rises from the site of the old castle of Leys and glides over the Hill of Banchory to Crathes Castle. It takes us back some four hundred years when the castle on the Loch of Leys was occupied by Lady Agnes, a proud independent widow and her son Alexander. When the boy was 17 they had a visit from a French relative named Sir Roger de Bernard. He had brought his daughter Bertha to Scotland for safe-keeping while he returned home to sort out his problems. Alexander and Bertha got on very well together and passed the days riding over the moors and visiting friends. Soon they were head over heels in love and everyone was delighted.

Everyone that is except Lady Agnes. She wanted her son to marry into the noble family of the Lords of Lorne. Alexander, however, was determined to ignore her disapproval. Then Lady Agnes hit on a drastic solution. While her son was away on business at Arbroath she poisoned their young guest with 'doctored' wine. Alexander returned home to find Bertha lying in the centre of the castle's main room on a bier.

Overcome with shock he went to sip some wine from a nearby goblet but Lady Agnes snatched it from his hand and threw the contents into the loch. Their eyes met and Alexander, horrified, realised what she had done. He loved Bertha yet at the same time couldn't bring himself to turn his own mother over to the authorities.

Some twelve months later while they were eating supper Sir Roger de Bernard arrived. News had recently reached him about Bertha's death and he accused Lady Agnes of murdering the girl. As he spoke the room turned very chilly and objects started moving about of their own accord. Then the widow was suddenly jolted upwards in her chair. Slowly she got to her feet screaming: "She comes, she comes." A few seconds later Lady Agnes was on the floor....dead.

Justice had been done. Alexander eventually married Janet Hamilton, kinswoman of Archbishop Hamilton. They decided that the old building would be best left to its sad memories and in 1533 work was started on construction of the present Crathes Castle.

The troubled servant

The Troubled Servant

Supernatural disturbances at a house near Aberdeen's Great Western Road ended abruptly with the discovery under floorboards of an envelope containing a postal order. The place had been empty for some time and a Mr Scarfe, who took a keen interest in things not of this world, was interested to hear of the ghostly goings-on while staying with some friends in the Granite City. He decided to find out more by spending a night there.

During the course of the evening the spirit of a servant girl appeared before him. She signalled Mr Scarfe to follow, then glided up the stairs. Needless to say he was terribly nervous but managed to stay cool. In the garret the ghost stopped at the hearth, pointed downwards for a few seconds then vanished into thin air.

Scarfe stayed just long enough to mark the spot. Next day he returned with the landlord who tore up the floorboards. All they found was a letter. At first it didn't appear to be anything of particular interest but as the two made further enquiries, an incredible story was unfolded.

They established that a few years earlier the house had been occupied by a fairly prosperous trades family who employed a servant girl called Anna Webb. Her description exactly fitted that of the ghost seen by Mr Scarfe. One morning Anna had been given some letters to post by the lady of the house but one containing a postal order never reached its destination. She was suspected of theft and threatened with prosecution. A continual barrage of questions from her employers drove Anna, a nervous lassie, to suicide.

At a subsequent inquiry into her death a note which she had written was produced. It stated: "As proof of my innocence I am going to hang myself. I never stole your letter and can only suppose it was lost in the post."

The discovery of the unopened letter would seem to suggest that Anna was completely innocent and the disturbances at the house finished the day those floorboards were lifted.

Burn her alive

Burn her Alive

A bite from a dog helped convict Helen Rogie of witchcraft. And the sentence of the court was: 'Burn her alive!'

She was known as the 'Witch of Findrack' and belonged to a coven which met regularly near Torphins. Rogie was arrested after cursing wealthy farmer John Mackie and his family. Their dog died suddenly, a few hours after biting her. A few days later Mrs Mackie fell and broke a leg. Then the daughter of the house died.

These, along with other mishaps and tragedies which befell neighbours, made the basis of Rogie's summons before the Assizes on charges of practising witchcraft. She received advance warning, presumably through supernatural sources, that a party of arresting officers were on their way to her cottage, and fled. The unfortunate lady managed to evade capture for some days before being traced to a cave in the hills. Earlier, a search of the cottage had found pictures of the people she had cursed, images cut in soft lead, strange writings, twisted wire and coloured threads.

At the Assizes, presided over by John Irvine of Pitmurchie in April, 1597, it was decided that Rogie be taken to the Gallows Hill at Craigour to be burnt. Expenses were agreed—66 pence to cover pay for the hangman and funds to provide twenty loads of peats, a boll of coal, four barrels of tar, four fathoms of rope and a stake.

BRIDGE OVER SLUGGAN WATER, NEAR BRAEMAR.

Banffshire's Green Lady

A ghost with a guilty conscience haunts a romantic valley in the coastal countryside of Banffshire. In life she was the wife of a local laird and for ten years had succeeded in keeping a grim secret from him.

Trouble began the day a travelling pedlar broke into their fruit garden. The laird was out at the time and the lady of the house sent an elderly ploughman to eject the intruder. A struggle developed between the two men and the force of one of the blows killed the pedlar.

The laird's wife was in a terrible panic and was about to recruit some other staff to go and find him when her eyes caught the dead man's pack. She liked the good things of life and the silks, velvets and satin which it contained made her forget the tragedy which had just taken place. The greedy woman started taking out the material for a closer look with the firm intention of stealing some of it when an even more exciting find was made...a treasure trove of gold coins.

There and then she decided to cover up the whole incident by splitting the goods and money with the ploughman. He was instructed to conceal the body in a place where no one would ever find it.

However this despicable act played more and more on her conscience as the years passed. But death a decade later did not bring total peace. The spirit of the laird's wife could not rest.

After her death she began appearing in the house before staff and outside in the fields workmen spotted her as well.

On one occasion she presented a young ploughman with a handful of silver coins. He put them in his pocket. But on going to spend them the astonished worker found that they were nothing more than slivers of slate.

About a year later the ghost — known as the Green Lady — appeared before a member of the household and told her about the hidden corpse and stolen treasure. A subsequent check of locations given confirmed the accuracy of the phantom's statements.

River Spirits

In the minds of our ancestors the link between water and magic did not end at wells. Each river was believed to have its own guardian spirit which was capable of transforming itself into shapes familiar to man. Most spirits appeared as horses and when in this form were known as "kelpies". Everyone knew, of course, that a river needed to have several victims through drowning every so often if it was to remain happy so to satisfy its thirst the kelpie would meet up with a weary foot traveller. No opposition would be offered when the inevitable attempt was made at a mount. Once the unsuspecting victim was safely aboard there was no way he could get off. The kelpie then went galloping off to the river and promptly deposited his prey into the swirling waters. The River Spey's spirit when in kelpie form appeared to the innocent onlooker as a beautiful white horse.

Spirits could also take on the appearance of people. That of the River Conon in Ross-shire used to appear "as a tall woman dressed in green, but distinguished chiefly by her withered meagre countenance, forever distorted by a malignant scowl." She was one of the most hostile spirits of all.

The tradition that rivers needed a victim from time to time to satisfy the spirit's thirst is noted in the following well-known rhyme:-
    Blood-thirsty Dee
    Each year needs three;
    But bonny Don
    She needes none.

There were times when the spirits did give help. After a basket-maker by the name of Farquharson drowned in the Dee his body could not be found. When the final searches were called off his widow took along the man's plaid, knelt down by the water's side, and prayed to the river to give her the corpse back. She then threw the plaid into the Dee. Next morning Farquharson was found. Wrapped around him was the plaid.

A similar story is recorded of the Don at Inverurie. Relatives anxious to recover the drowned body of a loved one were told by an old woman to place a biscuit in the water at the point where he met his end. They were then to follow its progress. The body would be found at the point where the biscuit sank. They followed her instructions carefully and it worked!

Lochs had spirits which made demands on inhabitants. The first lamb of the flock from several local farms had to be drowned in a small loch on the Aberdeenshire/Banffshire boundary. Any farmer who didn't keep his side of the bargain would find half of his sheep drowned before the close of the grazing season.

BALMORAL CASTLE FROM THE RIVER.